SUNGLASSES, MIXTAPES & MINISTRY

THE FLY CHICK'S GO-TO FOR GROWING IN FAITH

CHARISMA K. ADAMS

ISBN-13: 978-0-692-77889-0

Published by FlyyFaith Publishing
West Pam Beach, Florida

DEDICATION

To the chicks with more highlights in their hair than their bibles, the ones that wrote their life stories with tattoo guns, and the ones that are caught in the tension of religion and relationship, relax. You've got this!

CONTENTS

TRUST ISSUES   18

DON'T SLACK OFF   21

WILLING TO BE WEAK   25

DON'T BELIEVE THE LIE   28

YOU MAY FAIL, BUT GOD   31

NO WORRIES   34

NO SHORTCUTS   37

CRY NOW. LAUGH LATER.   41

WATCH GOD WORK   44

PERFECTLY IMPERFECT   47

GOSSIP THE GOSPEL   50

SALVATION ISN'T A SELFIE   53

INNER BEAUTY   56

IDENTIFIED BY LOVE   60

BEAR AND FORGIVE   63

FOR GOOD AND GLORY   66

DON'T TAKE THE CREDIT   69

LEARN TO LISTEN   72

LEFTOVERS   76

CONNECTION   79

NO EXCUSES	82
TAKEN	85
AUTHENTIC	88
RIDE OR DIE	91
FREE & LIGHT	94
HEART TRANSPLANT	97
MAKE UP YOUR MIND	100
UNSHAKEABLE	103
UNDIVIDED HEART	106
NOT ALONE	109
GET OUT OF THE OUTCOME	112
BETTER TOGETHER	115
MIND YOUR MIND	118
JESUS CHRIST, CEO	122
QUIET CONFIDENCE	125
CUT IT	128
GOD > ME	131
HEARTFELT PRAYERS	135
MAKE FAITH MUTUAL	138
GOD MODELED LOVIN'	141
EVEN GREATER	147

"Because there are too many things
for you to deal with.
Dying inside but outside
you looking fearless"

- excerpt "Keep ya head up" Tupac Shakur

"For every mountain
you brought me over
For every trial
you've seen me through
For every blessing
Hallelujah
For this I give you praise!"

-    excerpt "For Every Mountain" Kurt Carr

So here we are. Two young women on a journey toward living an abundant life in Christ. Okay, so maybe one of us is not so young, but you get my drift. Let me introduce myself. I am Charisma, a thirty-something wife and mother with a heart for women whose lives have been messy but who earnestly long to change their lifestyle, grow stronger in their faith, and deepen their relationship with God. Consider me your proverbial big sister, here to share some of my journey with you and help as best I can.

When I first realized that God was calling me into ministry, I was terrified. Not because I was afraid of where God would want me to go, but because I was afraid I'd have to reveal where I'd been. I'd been to some dark places, so I wasn't sure that I was ready to flip on the light switch of my past to show everyone the full extent of what God had saved me from (I also didn't want to embarrass my Mother). Frankly it was scary because deep down I didn't feel good enough and I still was hiding from the fact that I struggled in my thoughts and actions from time to time.

But the more I tried to just go on with my life, the louder the ringing of my call became. The more I tried to pretend that I could just go to church and serve my church family, the more I encountered women like me. Women who were lost, struggling, secretly longing, searching for answers, second guessing themselves, desiring more of God but not wanting to give up more of themselves in exchange. These women circulated in my mind all the time, even to the point that I couldn't sleep.

A few years ago I attended a live event hosted by Oprah Winfrey, and she asked us to think of someone that we love. We were to picture their face and then write down what we wished for their life. I thought of my fourteen-year-old daughter and wrote:

"What I wish for Zuri is exactly what I deeply desired but lacked the faith to wish for myself. I wish that she will have the confidence to pursue her highest calling and that she will feel safe and secure in who she is. I wish that when she discovers her purpose, she embraces it fully. I wish for her to be in love with her life's work and invigorated by her career. I wish her to become an optimistic, natural leader and a risk-taker for the cause of Christ. I wish her to be loved by her friends, supported by her family, and adored by a man that sets her soul on fire. I wish for her to be full of faith in God and fully surrendered to His will for her life."

Although this started out as my wish for Zuri, it soon became my wish for every woman that burdened my spirit. This is also my wish for you. But my wish cannot come to fruition unless you allow yourself to be open, transparent and vulnerable with God so that He can use your journey to grow you into the woman that He designed you to be. He has a divine purpose for you to walk in, and it starts here... right where you are, flipping through the pages of this book, unsure of what lies ahead but absolutely certain that you no longer want to stay where you are.

This isn't your ordinary *"take one in the morning before you start your day"* kind of devotional. This is a *"grab it because it's starting to get rough and real"* kind of thing. You don't have to read the devotions in order or even every day. Move as you are led and start with the ones you feel you need the most. Some may be exactly what you need in the moment and others the Holy Spirit may bring back to your memory later on down the road. Just make sure you take time to pause, reflect, and do the hard work.

I felt led to write this because I know what it's like to have rough days in your journey of spiritual growth. When I first started, I repeatedly made bad decisions simply because I didn't have a clear understanding of God, myself, or how this relationship between us should look. So if this book saves you one-quarter of what I experienced, then it has fulfilled its purpose.

The scriptures selected for this book are merely those that God led me to include based on the way He's equipped me. They are in no way all encompassing, but it is my prayer that each one reveals something to you that helps you add another brick to your foundation of faith.

Before you read this book, do a few things for me. First, grab you a pair of sunglasses. You will need them for the days you are walking around on the brink of tears. Next, create a good mix-tape so you can sing loudly and dance freely in gratitude to the rhythms of God's grace. Finally, open your heart to experience God as we take the first step toward intentionally growing our faith together.

C'mon! Let's get going.

TRUST ISSUES

The WORD:

"But blessed is the man who trusts me, God, **the woman who sticks with God**. *They're like trees replanted in Eden, putting down roots near the rivers—* **never a worry** *through the hottest of summers, never dropping a leaf,* **Serene and calm** *through droughts,* **bearing fresh fruit every season."**

Jeremiah 17:7-8, MSG

The WORK:

If you have ever been in a relationship with someone that has hurt you in a very personal way, the likelihood of you being able to trust that person ever again is probably low. Maybe it was a cheating ex-boyfriend or a backstabbing colleague. It may have even been the one person that assured you they wouldn't tell your secret. Nonetheless, the betrayal stung so badly that it ruined your ability to trust others. But regardless of what has happened with others in the past, we can always trust God. In fact, there are three important factors about Him that we must remember whenever we feel ourselves beginning to doubt His trustworthiness:

1. He is not a human, so lying is not in His nature. His word is always bond! (Num. 23:19).
2. He possesses the kind of power and authority that no one can even come

close to. There is absolutely nothing he cannot do. (Job 42:2).

3. He cares for you... deeply (1 Peter 5:7).

The more that you become convinced of these truths, the more your ability to trust Him will grow. It won't happen overnight, so don't get discouraged. You may have to keep reminding yourself over and over that he cannot lie and he cares more about you than any person you have dealt with previously. Don't let past relationships determine your level of trust in God; let God show you just how trustworthy He is.

Your WALK:

Search your heart to determine whether or not you have any issues with trusting God. If God highlights some areas to you, ask Him to heal those areas of your heart and to teach you more about the truth of who He really is.

DON'T SLACK OFF

The WORD:

*"**Run hard** and fast in the faith. Seize the eternal life, the life you were called to, the life you so fervently embraced in the presence of so many witnesses. **I'm charging you** before the life-giving God and before Christ, who took his stand before Pontius Pilate and didn't give an inch: Keep this command to the letter, and **don't slack off**. Our Master, Jesus Christ, is on his way. He'll show up right on time."*

1 Timothy 6:12-13, MSG

The WORK:

Our life of faith in Christ is often referred to as a race. Eternity with Jesus is the prize, and only those who persevere all the way to the end are considered winners. Sounds simple enough, right? Well, it is at first.

When most of us first come into a relationship with Christ, we have this fiery passion burning deep in our soul that fuels our desire to totally change our lifestyles and pursue a growing relationship with Him. In those early days, you may feel like this race is going to be easy and find yourself sprinting with great speed. But as time goes on and hurdles appear, our fire begins to dwindle. We aren't as anxious to attend church activities. We start sleeping in on Sunday mornings and most of us that had a great start in the beginning, begin to drop out of the race altogether. We all to quickly discover that what appeared to be a sprint actually is a marathon and we didn't have enough fuel to make the distance.

This is why it's incredibly important that we don't rely on that initial fire to sustain us for the entire race. We must find a group of believers that we can connect to so that we may continually be refueled. We need to plan to take a path that includes refueling stations along the way like weekend worship services, bible studies, small groups, prayer time, journaling, meditation, etc. It is through maintaining a full tank that you will be able to make it to the finish line.

Your WALK:

Picture Jesus waiting at the finish line for you with open arms and a gold medal. Imagine the overwhelming sense of accomplishment that you'll feel on that day. Whenever the race begins to get hard, remember to look at Jesus, and let your desire to please Him and hear "well done" get you through.

PRAYER PAUSE

God, I understand that this journey may

require more from me than I've given to

anything before in my life. It's scary to even

think of sacrificing at that level. But I can admit

that my way of doing things hasn't been

working and I really believe you love me and

have a better plan for my life than I can

probably even envision. I'm ready. I'm really

ready this time. I want to grow our relationship

and I am going to start right now, right here by

spending more time with you. Amen.

WILLING TO BE WEAK

The WORD:

*"My **grace** is enough; it's **all you need**. My strength comes into its own in your weakness. Once I heard that, I was glad to let it happen. I quit focusing on the handicap and began appreciating the gift. It was a case of Christ's strength **moving in on my weakness**. Now I take limitations in stride, and with good cheer, these limitations that cut me down to size—abuse, accidents, opposition, bad breaks. I just let **Christ take over**! And so the weaker I get, the stronger I become."*

2 Corinthians 12:9-10, MSG

The WORK:

Have you ever had the flu or any other kind of illness that left you so weak and tired you could barely get out of bed? It's the worst feeling, right? No one likes feeling weak. Weakness is typically accompanied by a sense of helplessness, uselessness or even self-pity, none of which are ideal.

God made women to be incredibly strong forces on this earth, and that can be to our benefit, but sometimes it can also be to our detriment because we will often try to rely on our own strength to accomplish everything. But we are only human, and it is impossible for us please God simply through our own strength. If we want to be able to please a supernatural God, we're going to need supernatural strength. That strength is found in Jesus.

The beautiful thing about our relationship with Christ is that He loves those moments when we're so weak that His strength can shine through us. He loves to be able to lift us up when we're tired and to carry us on His shoulders when we feel like we can't walk anymore. But He will never force us to depend on Him. All that He waits for is for us to let Him take over.

This may be hard for many of us women who suffer from the "Superwoman Syndrome". We feel that we can do it all, be it all and help everyone. This way of living only burns us out more quickly and ensures that we are not giving our best selves to anyone. We have to learn to be willing to be weak so that God's grace can have an area to enter in and help us.

Your WALK:

Make a list of the areas where you feel weak today (i.e. specific relationships, prayer, devotional life, etc.) and ask God to take each situation and be strong in your weakness.

DON'T BELIEVE THE LIE

The WORD:

*"For **all** have sinned and **fall short** of the glory of God."*

Romans 3:23, NIV

The WORK:

When you take a look around at the family of believers that you have become a part of, it may be a bit intimidating at first. Maybe you look at the women in the church and the way they live their lives, and like I did, you feel like you don't measure up. Don't believe the lie.

Everyone struggles with sin. That's the reality of the Christian life for every single believer in this world. Yes, God has set us free from the power of sin, but because our spirits still reside in these earthly bodies that are naturally filled with wickedness, it's a constant, daily struggle to keep our desires in line with God's will. So you may be doing just fine in your walk with God, when something comes along out of the blue to trip you up. It can be an old boyfriend when you are feeling lonely, an invite to the club when you are bored, or even an offer of drugs or alcohol when you are battling trying to overcome addiction. But just because you stumble doesn't mean you're out of the race.

One of the most beautiful aspects of living a life in Christ is that when we fall down, the only thing that is required is that we come to Him in repentance, get back up and keep on going. We don't have to put ourselves in timeout or beat ourselves up for being "bad Christians". Jesus doesn't condemn us, so why do we continually condemn ourselves? It's simply because we've believed the lie that the enemy whispered in our ear that we are the only one struggling like this.

Your WALK:

If you ever feel the need to condemn yourself because of a mistake that you've made, call another sister and admit where you have been struggling. I guarantee you will discover you aren't alone. Ask her for encouragement or prayer and continue to press on.

YOU MAY FAIL, BUT GOD

The WORD:

*"**My flesh** and my heart **may fail**, but **God is the strength** of my heart and my portion forever."*

Psalms 73:26, ESV

The WORK:

When we come face-to-face with the reality of how weak we are as human beings, it can be a tough pill to swallow. Our spirit may want so desperately to please God, but it just seems like our actions refuse to get on the same page and instead keep leading us into trouble. Just thank God that our success in this lifestyle doesn't depend on us, but on the one who lives inside of us!

You may know the famous story of Derek Redmond, an Olympic runner who tore his hamstring during one of his races. Overcome with a rock solid determination to never quit, he continued hobbling towards the finish line. Derek's father ran onto the track from the sidelines and held his son to support him as they walked together towards the finish line. He didn't give up just because he got injured. That is such a perfect picture of our relationship with our heavenly Father and the way He carries us when our heart and flesh give out on us. As long as we purpose in our hearts that quitting isn't an option, God will come and meet us right where we are in order to walk with us.

It can't be said enough that there are going to be times that you will stumble and fall, but God is the strength of our walk. He will never let go of us until He has finished the good work that He began in us.

Your WALK:

Imagine the vast amount of strength your heavenly Father possesses. Now picture that same amount of strength dwelling inside of you, even on your weakest days. Let that be a constant reminder to you of what it means to have Christ as your strength, and then tap into it!

NO WORRIES

The WORD:

"Don't fret or worry. **Instead of worrying, pray**. Let petitions and praises shape your worries into prayers, letting God know your concerns. Before you know it, a sense of **God's wholeness**, everything coming together for good, **will come and settle you down**. It's wonderful what happens when Christ displaces worry at the center of your life."

Philippians 4:6-7, MSG

The WORK:

Worry is such an easy habit for Christians and non-Christians alike to fall into. It's the only response that seems to make sense to us when something is out of our control. But as natural as it may seem, it is something that the Bible repeatedly instructs us to refrain from.

Bible teacher Margaret Feinberg penned the quote, "Worry is a subtle way of telling God that He's fallen asleep at the wheel and that things aren't under His authority, but ours." When you think about worry this way, it's easy to see why it is something that God discourages. At the very heart of our faith should be the belief that nothing is too difficult for God. Worry displays the exact opposite.

The tricky bit about allowing ourselves to get into a mindset of worry is that it not only influences our thought lives, but it can have a negative effect on our prayer lives as well.

Instead of praying from a position of faith, we pray from a position of fear. We approach him as timid beggars unsure if He cares enough to intervene instead of as beloved daughters. If you really want to see God move in response to your needs and prayer requests, try approaching Him as someone who really believes that He's got everything under control.

Your WALK:

Pay close attention to the words you speak in your personal prayer life. Take note of the times that you pray out of fear or doubt, and actively work to rephrase your prayers to express your firm belief that God is in control. Even a simple shift in your prayer language can give you a great faith boost!

NO SHORTCUTS

The WORD:

*"Consider it a sheer gift, friends, when tests and challenges come at you from all sides. You know that **under pressure**, your faith-life is forced into the open and shows its true colors. So **don't try to get out** of anything **prematurely**. Let it do its work **so you become mature** and well-developed, not deficient in any way."*

James 1:2-4, MSG

The WORK:

There's a misconception among some new believers that once you become a Christian, life is smooth sailing from then on out. The truth is that life as a Christian is actually quite the opposite. Jesus promised us that we would walk through many troubles, that we would be hated throughout the world for our faith in Him, and that we would have to undergo great suffering.

Now, the last word that most of us would use to describe this kind of life is "gift", and yet that's the perspective we're encouraged to adopt. Why? Because as much as going through such situations will not feel pleasant at the time, the goal is not to look at your present suffering, but to look ahead to what that suffering will produce in your character. Our goal is to look at how each trial and circumstance can make us better, build our faith and even strengthen our prayer lives.

When you go through difficult times your faith is tested. But more importantly the hidden flaws in our character are revealed. It isn't until you are provoked that you discover your anger issues. When you are hurt, you can see how you struggle with unforgiveness. The more you endure, the more God can mature you in your faith.

Your WALK:

The next time you find yourself in the middle of a bad situation, try to remove your focus from the situation at hand and focus instead on what good can come of it. You may even try writing this down on the front and back of an index card. On one side write what you are experiencing and on the back list all of the good things it can produce in your character and life. God will work every situation together for our good; we just need the faith to believe.

PRAYER PAUSE

Father, *thank you for your forgiveness. Thank you for removing my sins from me and casting them into the sea of forgetfulness. Now help me to forgive myself for every mistake and wrong action that I have committed against myself and others. Forgive me for doubting and denying that I am a daughter of the Most High God and living beneath my God given right. I forgive myself for undermining the power of your love in my life by remaining in unhealthy relationships. I release myself from the guilt and shame that is associated with past mistakes and errors. I will not allow my past to hold me any longer. I thank you that when you set your daughters free, we are totally free.*

Amen.

CRY NOW. LAUGH LATER.

The WORD:

*"No **discipline** **is** enjoyable while it is happening—it's **painful**! But **afterward** there will be a **peaceful harvest** of right living for those who are trained in this way."*

Hebrews 12:11, NLT

The WORK:

When you were a kid, if you did something wrong, your parents may have disciplined you by putting you in time out, grounding you, or by spanking you. In that particular moment, the thoughts that went through your head were undoubtedly unpleasant. Maybe you thought your parents were unfair, maybe you thought they hated you, or maybe you even hated them. That's human nature. We don't like discipline.

Believe it or not, this is also the way we tend to respond to God when He disciplines us. When God has to humble us by not allowing us to get a certain thing we've been asking for or by taking us down a route that is different than the one we would have chosen for ourselves, we spiritually cross our arms, pout and get upset. We don't like discipline.

Discipline is emotionally painful even if not

physically and requires determination to endure it. But the thing that we need to remember is that God disciplines those that He loves (Heb. 12:6). Just as our parents disciplined us in order to make us better, so the Lord disciplines us to make us more like His Son, Jesus. Discipline helps cut away the F.A.T. (Future Altering Things). The things that if left unattended in us and permitted to grow will undoubtedly change the trajectory of our lives. We have the choice to either refuse to accept it or to learn to love it. Just don't forget that discipline is always to shape your destiny.

Your WALK:

There is always a reason why the Lord disciplines us. It's usually because there's something He sees that we can't yet. If you ever find yourself being disciplined, ask Him what He's trying to teach you, then yield yourself to His method of instruction.

WATCH GOD WORK

The WORD:

*"If people can't **see what God** is doing, they stumble all over themselves; but when they attend to what he **reveals**, they are most **blessed**."*

Proverbs 29:18, MSG

The WORK:

No matter what sphere of influence you're in—
whether it's your personal life, your work
environment, an educational setting, and so
on—goal setting is of the utmost importance.
After all, it's important that you know which
direction you're supposed to be heading before
you take your first step. Notice I said *direction*
and not *destination*, right?   Our natural
inclination is to desire to see the destination
before we move. But that's not how God works.
We don't usually get to know where we will end
up but since our steps are ordered, God will
always reveal the direction of the first step.

As Christians, the Lord gives each of us a
vision, or an overall goal, for different areas of
our lives. Of course He has given all believers
a   general   goal,   to   keep   themselves
untarnished from the world (James 1:27), but
to each individual He also gives a special
vision. Without such vision, we are left to

stumble around in the dark, groping to find some sort of meaning for our lives.

When God reveals to us the vision that He has for our lives, and when we begin to pursue that vision, we begin to experience the blessings of the Lord and really see His best work. There is an immense sense of peace and joy that fills the heart of those who know that where they are is exactly where God wants them to be. Do you have that assurance?

Your WALK:

If you currently do not know what vision the Lord has for you, ask the Lord to reveal it to you. Take note of the passions He has planted in your heart since childhood, and open yourself for a new adventure!

PERFECTLY IMPERFECT

The WORD:

*"Farmers who wait for perfect weather never **plant**. If they watch every cloud, they never **harvest**."*

Ecclesiastes 11:4, NLT

The WORK:

When we have to make decisions, whether big or small, we often like to wait until the conditions are not just favorable, but perfect. As teens, most of us probably pre-determined the perfect age for marriage and children, and as adults, we probably still adhere to those timetables. There are even some people that claim they need to experience the perfect conditions in their lives before they come to Jesus.

As much as it may seem right for us to want to make sure we have "all our ducks" in a row before we make a decision, it is almost impossible for us to truly know what is perfect and what is not. Our vision and understanding of any given situation are at best, limited.

The only person whose timing is perfect is God. He is the only one who can see the end from the beginning; the present, past, and future. He even knows all of the possible outcomes from every decision we could possibly make. If that is the case, why do we still choose our timing over God's? We must shift our perspective from what we can see and what we think we know to inquire of someone who already knows all things.

Waiting for everything to align perfectly before you step out on a new opportunity, open your heart to a potential mate, purchase your first home, or even start your business almost always ensures you miss God's ability to work perfectly in the imperfect.

Your WALK:

Is there a particular area in your life where you are waiting for the perfect timing or conditions? Write them down and ask the Lord for direction on what to do and when to do it. Then go ahead and jump! You won't regret it.

GOSSIP THE GOSPEL

The WORD:

*"Then he said, "**Go into the world**. Go **everywhere** and **announce** the Message of God's good news **to one and all**.*

Mark 16:15, MSG

The WORK:

When we hear some juicy news, the first thing we usually get the urge to do is to run and tell someone. We are the queens of, "I promise won't tell anyone", as you are already rehearsing the story for replay in your mind. Or what about the photo album we all have nearly a quarter full of screenshots? In most cases you share the news with someone really close to you, but if it's really good, you're tempted to shout your news to the world.

Why isn't this the reaction we have for good news? Why don't we run and gossip about all of the great things that God has done for us? This is exactly how we should respond when we experience the salvation of Jesus. Our heart's desire should be to "go tell it on the mountain" and to let everyone know what He has done for us. Only you know exactly what Jesus has set you free from or brought you through. Only you can share the story of what you felt in your heart the moment that Jesus walked into it. But usually we are reluctant to do so because of the accountability that comes along with testimony. When you share what God has delivered you from, you know they are watching you now, right? Waiting for the next slip up, waiting for the next curse word, watching if you pour that drink. Don't allow your fear of your weakness at this point in your walk to stop you from glorifying God in your life. Be transparent but be honest. Other women are waiting to be set free from their own struggles and your testimony is what helps them. (Rev 12:11) Be on the lookout for opportunities to share your testimony with those in your spheres of influence.

Your WALK:

Ask the Lord to help you identify someone that you can share your story with. No one has a story like yours, so use your story to bring praise and glory to God like only you can!

SERVING ISN'T A SELFIE

The WORD:

*"Each of you should **use** whatever **gift** you have received **to serve** others, as faithful stewards of God's grace in its various forms."*

1 Peter 4:10, NIV

The WORK:

Many of us start out believing that our Christian walk is about our own spiritual journey, but it's actually more about how God wants to work through us to help others along the way. In that wise, anything that we receive from Christ is to be shared with others, from our personal testimony of salvation to our unique talents and gifts.

Take for instance the story of Joseph in the Bible. God chose him to become second in command in all of Egypt, one of the strongest nations in the world at the time. When it was all said and done, Joseph acknowledged that he had only been given such a position for the sake of God's people; not because he deserved it or because he was the most qualified (Genesis 45:5-8).

This must be our response as well. Your story of salvation is a prime example of how others gave. Jesus first gave His life to make a way for you to approach the Father, and then someone undoubtedly gave of his or her time to share this message with you to help you get to the point of salvation. Now it's your turn. To whom will you give?

Jesus chose twelve people to walk alongside him on his Earthly journey. He used His gifts to serve them. He led them, healed them, taught them, corrected them, prayed for them, and equipped them. He poured out all that he had into the people he did life with. Jesus turned the lens of life around and focused His on serving others instead of himself. Are you doing the same or taking selfies with yours?

Your WALK:

Take some time to identify your gifts. Make a list of them, take note of the many ways you can use those gifts to serve others, and then get to it!

INNER BEAUTY

The WORD:

*"Your **adornment** must not be merely external- -braiding the hair, and wearing gold jewelry, or putting on dresses; but let it be the hidden person of the heart, with the **imperishable** quality of a **gentle and quiet spirit**, which is precious in the sight of God."*

1 Peter 3:3-4, NASB

The WORK:

We live in a culture where appearance is everything. Just scroll through any form of social media or flip through any magazine, and you'll quickly see that it is primarily centered on the hottest looks, brands, and trends, all of which most of the female population totally eats up.

But God's definition of beauty is countercultural. According to Him, the way we decorate and accessorize ourselves has nothing to do with our beauty. It's what's on the inside that matters. As corny or cliché as that may sound, it's true. Have you ever met a guy who physically didn't appeal to you initially? However, the more you got to know him and discover admirable qualities in his personality, the more attractive he become to you, right?

None of us have ever seen God, and yet we believe that He is beautiful. If you closed your eyes right now and pictured God, He'd be handsome I'm sure. To prove this point further, visualize Satan. Exactly!

How can we know that God is beautiful or Satan is ugly for that matter? Because we know their hearts. This is the same standard by which our beauty should be judged; so let the beauty of your inner spirit give the world an authentic measure of real beauty. It's possible that the more we as believers emphasize the importance of inner beauty through our actions, music, magazines, books and social media, the world can be influenced by us to start to dig beneath the surface.

Your WALK:

Write down the external qualities that you deem beautiful about yourself. Now draw a line through each one and replace with an inner quality that you'd like to cultivate more in your life. Seek ways to develop the inner qualities.

PRAYER PAUSE

Father, *I know I was hand crafted to fulfill a specific purpose on this earth. Open my heart and mind to receive and understand your MASTER plan for my life. I lay down at your feet every plan that I have conceived. Reveal the gifts and talents that you have invested in me for your Kingdom. Surround me with others who are called to help me identify and grow in my gifts. As iron sharpens iron, lead me to those who will serve as mentors to guide me through this journey of discovering and walking in my purpose. As daily distractions come to take my attention away from my pursuit of you, center me in your glorious plan and anchor my heart and mind in Your Word. Amen.*

IDENTIFIED BY LOVE

The WORD:

*"A new command I give you: Love one another. As **I** **have** **loved** **you**, so you must love one another. By this **everyone will know** that you are my disciples, if* ***you love one another.****"*

John 13:34-35, NIV

The WORK:

In the Old Testament the Israelites were given a very long list of rules that they had to follow in order to prove to the world that they were, in fact, the children of God. This list governed the way they dressed, what they ate, who they hung out with, and much more.

When Jesus came along, hundreds of years later, He flipped everything upside down. He said, "Instead of giving you a list of laws to follow, let me break it down into three words: love one another." Love replaces any other commandment, because it is the foundation to every commandment.

If you love God, you will not have to be monitored to do what is right in His eyes. You will be self-motivated to please Him. If you love yourself, you won't abuse your body with drugs and alcohol or allow boyfriends to come and enjoy your body at their leisure without a commitment of marriage. If you love those around you, you won't feel inclined to steal from them, lie to them, or commit any kind of heinous crime against them, so it stands to reason that if your main priority is to love, not only will you keep away from wicked things, but you will pursue the loving nature of Christ. You will effectively become identified as daughters of Christ by which God can show His love to the world. No one will ever have to ask if you are a follower of Christ. They will easily identify you because of the love that flows freely throughout your life in a world filled with hatred.

Your WALK:

Is love the guiding force behind all of your thoughts, words, and actions to others? As you go throughout your day, ask yourself this question after each interaction and challenge yourself to do all things in love so the world can see that you are, in fact, a child of God.

BEAR AND FORGIVE

The WORD:

"**Bear with each other** and **forgive one another** if any of you has a grievance against someone. Forgive as the Lord forgave you."

Colossians 3:13, NIV

The WORK:

As Jesus hung from the cross, having been placed there by those who once claimed to love Him, He cried out: "Father, forgive them, for they know not what they do." Jesus could have asked God for anything in that moment, and God probably would have given it to Him, but His only request was that the Father wouldn't hold anything against those that murdered His son.

This is undoubtedly the most powerful example of forgiveness in the entire Bible, and like any example, it was given to us so that we can learn from it and follow it. As believers, we are not meant to walk around with a chip on our shoulder. We are to show the world what it means to live as one who has been set free not only from the power of sin, but from the pain of unforgiveness.

Forgiveness isn't easy, but nothing Jesus has

called us to is. Forgiveness often causes us to feel like we are letting the person off the hook and that they got away with it. Revenge, paying them back or getting even should never be the aim for us as believers. Although that may have been how we lived before. Forgiveness is the way we laugh at the enemy's attempt to do us harm. We can laugh because we have the assurance that no matter what he conjures up against us, it won't work. (Isa 54:17) Forgiveness is the evidence that you believe in your heart that the weapon really didn't work.

Your WALK:

As you were reading this, you probably immediately recalled some people in your life that you need to forgive. Whatever the issue, bring it to the Lord and ask Him to give you the strength you need to take that first step towards letting it go. Now take at least one small step whether it's a phone call or a smile.

FOR GOOD AND GLORY

The WORD:

*"But I have raised you up for this very purpose, that I might **show** you **my power** and that my **name** might be **proclaimed** in all the earth."*

Exodus 9:16, NIV

The WORK:

You probably already know that God has a plan for your life, but have you ever stopped to think about the fact that God also has a plan for the entirety of mankind, and your story is only a small part of a bigger picture? Our lives are like a single beat in an elaborate song that He has been mastering together for ages.

Although God has promised to work everything together for our good, His main objective is to bring glory to Himself. He wants the world to know who He is and the full extent of His power and love. To that end, sometimes He will make choices that don't make sense to us. For instance, would you believe that today's scripture was not spoken to a righteous person but to Pharaoh, the guy who refused to let God's people free from slavery?

God raises up whom He chooses, when He chooses, but always for the same reason: His glory. It may not make any sense to us in the moment, but what we can believe is that in the end He will receive glory from it. It was part of His plan all along.

The most challenging part in receiving this word is that we want everything to feel good. When he walks out His purposes through your yielded life, oftentimes it may not feel good but it is always for good.

Your WALK:

Whenever situations arise in your life that cause you to doubt God's ability to work everything together for the best possible good, remember that He is committed to working everything out for your good and His glory.

DON'T TAKE THE CREDIT

The WORD:

"If you start thinking to yourselves, "I did all this. And all by myself. I'm rich. It's all mine!"— well, think again. **Remember** *that God, your* **God, gave you** *the strength to produce all* **this wealth** *so as to confirm the covenant that he promised to your ancestors—as it is today."*

Deuteronomy 8:18, MSG

The WORK:

One of the biggest issues mankind has faced since the beginning of time is pride. It's what caused Satan to fall from heaven, and it's what causes us to fall out of line with God's will time and time again. Pride makes us think more of ourselves and blinds us from the truth.

It is very easy to take credit for the job that God gave us and attribute it to our degree or skills. It is common to believe that raise or bonus is the result of our hard work. That's only partly true. We were able to work hard only because God gave us the strength. That bright idea for that new product came from God too. We can't brag about all we've done as if we did it alone. Our boast must be only of the amazing power of God living inside of us.

Before we get to such a place, where God has to humble us in a very humiliating way, we ought to humble ourselves first. Nothing that we have or have done could be possible without God, because all things come from Him. There is nothing tangible or intangible, seen or unseen that cannot be attributed to the power of God. We would do well to remember that.

It doesn't just stop with us bragging differently. This scripture reminds us that we should spend differently too. Our wealth and success is to help God continue to reach more people and for us to impact more lives with His love and message, not to accumulate more flyness in our closets and garages.

Your WALK:

Pride can sneak up on us in various ways, but its main objective is to glorify self. Ask yourself if you've allowed pride to gain power in your life. If you have, humble yourself before the Lord. From this day forward seek ways to honor and serve God more with your money.

LEARN TO LISTEN

The WORD:

*"**Trust God** from the bottom of your heart; don't try to figure out everything on your own. **Listen for God**'s voice in everything you do, everywhere you go; he's the one who **will keep you on track**."*

Proverbs 3:5-6, MSG

The WORK:

Life can throw a number of curveballs at us, and it's natural for us to want to figure out how to circumnavigate around the obstacles on our own. For women especially, we like to make plans, and just in case those plans don't work, we've got a handy dandy set of back-up plans for our plans.

As admirable as this quality may be, it can get us into trouble when it comes to our ability to listen to God. Oftentimes we'll only listen when we don't immediately have an answer or solution, but if we feel that God isn't moving fast enough, we'll snatch that thing back in a heartbeat and try to figure it out on our own.

If you are anything like me, you probably prefer to talk than listen anyway. The issue with this type of living is found in this scripture; you end up off track. We are so busy talking and walking through our life that we haven't even checked back with our compass (Christ) to make sure we are still headed in the right direction.

God promised that His aim was to prosper us and not to harm us (Jer. 29:11), so if we really claim to trust Him, we need to remove our hands from the wheel and listen to the voice whispering, "This is the way you should go. Walk in it."

Your WALK:

What areas of your life have you not totally surrendered to the leading of God yet? Where are you being driven by your own ideas of success and not surrendered to the voice of the Spirit of God? Once you have identified them, release them to the Lord in your heart with the belief that He's got it all under control, and be sure not to pick them back up again!

PRAYER PAUSE

Lord, *increase my ability to believe that which you have spoken over my life is true. Help me to look beyond my current circumstances and shortcomings and view my life through your lens. Remove the blinders of doubt and disappointment and give me insight to see myself how you see me. Give me grace to seek your face daily. In times of doubt when I feel inadequate, empower me to stand on your word in agreement with what you say that I can do. My desire is to stand in faith and follow you. The results are in your hands. As I meditate on your word, I believe my faith will increase causing massive growth in every area of my life. Amen*

LEFTOVERS

The WORD:

*"And **God will generously provide** all you need. Then you will always have everything you need and plenty left over to **share with others**."*

2 Corinthians 9:8 NLT

The WORK:

Everyday when I cook dinner I prepare enough food for my family of four. I always know its enough for all of us because I generally can anticipate the portions that each of us will eat. However, there are days when my husband has had a hearty lunch and isn't that hungry for dinner or one of the children ate something on the way home from sports practice. These days always leave us with leftovers after we have taken what we've needed. We usually just pack it away in the fridge for another day.

Like our own children, as daughters of the King of all Kings, we have the promise that we will always be taken care of. He has assured us that we need not ever worry about our basic needs. (Matt 6:31-32) But our promise doesn't stop there. He has committed to give us much more.

Now, when God blesses us with more, it's not

for us to pack away like yesterday's leftovers or even to use on ourselves, but to share with others. Remember, the same degree that He has been generous towards us, we should show generosity towards others.

If we look over our lives I am certain we will find tons of leftovers just sitting around. Leftover clothes you haven't worn in ages, leftover money from unexpected sources, or even leftover time from a cancelled appointment are all things that can be shared with someone in need.

Your WALK:

How has God generously blessed you? In what ways can you generously give to those around you? Make a point to look for ways to be a blessing to others whenever you receive blessings from God.

CONNECTION

The WORD:

*"**Remain in me**, as I also remain in you. No branch can bear fruit by itself; it must remain in the vine. Neither can you bear fruit unless you remain in me. "I am the vine; you are the branches. If you remain in me and I in you, **you will bear much fruit**; apart from me you can do nothing."*

John 15:4-5, NIV

The WORK:

Anyone who has received Christ into his or her hearts has also received the Holy Spirit as an internal guide. The easiest way to tell that someone has the Holy Spirit dwelling inside of them is to pay attention to the kind of fruit they bear.

Good deeds = good fruit
Bad deeds = bad fruit

Unless we remain in Christ, there is no way that we can produce good fruit. Any piece of fruit that is removed from its branch will quickly begin to ripen and decompose, and in the same way, if we try to do good apart from Christ, our actions will most likely be fueled by selfish ambition rather than meekness or pride rather than humility.

The longer a piece of fruit is attached to the branch, the more nutrients it can draw. Likewise, we can do nothing apart from Christ, so we must stay connected to the vine. It is the only way to continue to receive the vitamins and nutrients we need to produce good fruit.

Although we often feel that our lack of connection goes unnoticed and we can "fake it until we make it", that just isn't true. Like any other fruit, the rotting starts on the inside so you will feel it before anyone else. You will begin to notice things like you are more irritable, you have no desire to attend church or small group, or you are finding it more difficult to pray. If you don't reconnect quickly, others will begin to see it too as it begins to spread outward through your actions.

Your WALK:

Have you started feeling differently? Look back over your calendar and see if you notice inconsistencies in your connection time. Start back connecting with God so you can produce the kind of fruit that tastes sweet to the soul.

NO EXCUSES

The WORD:

*"But that's no life for you. **You learned Christ**! My assumption is that you have paid careful attention to him, been well **instructed in the truth** precisely as we have it in Jesus. Since, then, we **do not have the excuse of ignorance**, everything—and I do mean everything—connected with that old way of life has to go. It's rotten through and through. Get rid of it! And then take on an entirely **new way of life**—a God-fashioned life, a life renewed from the inside and working itself into your conduct as God accurately reproduces his character in you."*

Ephesians 4:22-24, MSG

The WORK:

Before you came to know Christ, there was a certain way you spoke, a certain way you acted, and a certain way your mind worked. Everything was controlled by your flesh, which is rotten through and through. We refer to that as your old self, because it is who you *were* until Jesus stepped into your heart.

Now with Jesus dwelling inside, His very nature saturates your own and completely transforms your life, changing the way you speak, act, and think. In that wise, Christianity becomes more than just following a bunch of rules in order to be a good person, but it becomes about allowing the purity of Christ to influence every decision you make.

Every day of your life, God is working to make you more like His Son. At the same time, the enemy is working to tempt you to revert back to your old nature. He lures you with smoke and mirrors and makes everything behind you appear to be everything you've ever wanted. As much as your flesh may want to go back, you know the truth. You know that everything connected with your old way of life is not worth going back to no matter how hard your current walk feels. You know that Jesus is worth it. Don't let the enemy trick you into believing otherwise.

Your WALK:

Whenever you feel tempted to go back to your old ways, remember that Christ was tempted by the enemy but overcame through the Word of God (Matt. 4:1-11). Find scriptures that relate to your specific areas of temptation and use them to combat the lies of the enemy.

TAKEN

The WORD:

*"With the arrival of **Jesus**, the Messiah, that fateful dilemma is resolved. Those who enter into Christ's being-here-for-us no longer have to live under a continuous, low-lying black cloud. A **new power is in operation**. The Spirit of life in Christ, like a strong wind, has magnificently cleared the air, **freeing you** from a fated lifetime of brutal tyranny at the hands of sin and death."*

Romans 8:1-2, MSG

The WORK:

I loved the movie "Taken". Liam Neeson's daughter was kidnapped and held hostage by some sex traffickers and he had to rescue her before she officially became a slave. Although at the start he seemed like a normal doting dad, his love for her revealed a passionate drive that fueled him to pursue after her relentlessly. The reality of the matter is that we were once in her position ourselves.

As kidnapped daughters and slaves to sin, the enemy held us captive. Even if we wanted to do the right thing, the ruler of our flesh had all authority to overrule our desires and force us to do his dirty work. But the moment that you called for your Father, he began to pursue after you with a force that was no match for the enemy. He broke the power that Satan had over your life and set you free.

The problem is that sometimes we don't realize that we've been set free. We sit in our abandoned warehouses, completely unaware that the chains have already been undone, simply because we believe that the power of sin is too strong to overcome. But the truth is that greater is He that is in us that he that is in the world (1 John 4:4). It's just up to us to start to live like it we've been rescued and set free.

Your WALK:

Are there areas of your life where you still live as though you're in bondage? Do you still feel enslaved to old behaviors and trains of thought? Those things don't have any power over you anymore, so declare that truth! Whenever they try to arise and say anything different, speak the truth, "I am free."

AUTHENTIC

The WORD:

*"So **be content with who you are**, and don't put on airs. **God's strong hand is on you**; he'll promote you at the right time."*

1 Peter 5:6, MSG

The WORK:

We're all looking for promotions in one way or another. Whether it's in the sphere of work, social status, or reputation, it's natural for us to want to feel respected and admired. Unfortunately, many people seem to think that the best way to achieve that is through either glorifying themselves or pretending to be something they're not.

But that is not the way of the kingdom. The way of the kingdom is one of humility and service. If there's one thing God doesn't like, it's when people sing their own praises. Actually, in Jesus' Sermon on the Mount, there's nearly a whole chapter (Matthew 6) dedicated to what kind of rewards are in store for such people: the praise of men is all they get. They get nothing from God.

When we do good or praiseworthy things, it can be hard to keep from wanting to tell the world how awesome we are, but if we pursue the praise of men, we will assuredly miss out on the blessings of God. God looks for the ones that everyone else looks over; the ones who do praiseworthy things in secret, and He exalts them above everyone else. He rewards and blesses them in public. They are like the people who receive the "Unsung Hero" awards. They are motivated by the cause, not the applause. Humble yourself in His sight, then He will lift you up.

Your WALK:

Read Matthew 6 to gain more insight about God's expectations of us in regards to humility, and begin to incorporate these principles into your own lifestyle.

The WORD:

*"So if you find **life difficult** because you're doing what God said, **take it in stride**. **Trust him**. He knows what he's doing, and he'll keep on doing it."*
1 Peter 4:19, MSG

The WORK:

For most of us, if we encounter danger, we're going to turn and run the other way. Human instinct is to get as far away from negative situations as possible. It's understandable, then, that whenever we face problems as Christians, we want to run away. Sometimes it can be hard to understand God's method in the midst of madness.

The cool thing about Jesus though, is that He prepared us for this. When people would tell Jesus they wanted to be His followers in the Bible, it's like He would say, "Are you sure? You will have to give up everything. Also, the whole world will hate you because you are riding with me now".

In response, some people chose to go the

other way, while others said, "Yes, Lord. I'll risk it all because I believe in you and your cause that much. I trust you." Most of us have at least one friend or family member that we are willing to roll with like that. There is one that we consider our "ride-or-die" and we'd go through the fire with them. As believers we must remember that the path of righteousness comes with much resistance. That's par for the course, but we also have the great promise that the sovereign God is with us, but we must make the difficult choice to continue to ride with Him against all odds.

Your WALK:

When you make difficult choices to serve God remind yourself of why following Jesus is so important and find comfort that in the end the reward will be greater than the loss.

FREE & LIGHT

The WORD:

"Are you tired? Worn out? Burned out on religion? **Come** *to me.* **Get away with me** *and you'll recover your life. I'll show you how to take a real rest. Walk with me and work with me—watch how I do it.* **Learn the unforced rhythms of grace.** *I won't lay anything heavy or ill-fitting on you. Keep company with me and you'll* **learn to live freely and lightly.**"

Matthew 11:28-30, MSG

The WORK:

Burn out. We all face it sooner or later. It's that moment when all of life's responsibilities pile up on your shoulders to the point that you feel too tired or too weak to keep going. Regardless of how you get to that point—whether through not knowing how to say no or just a desire to be involved in a lot of things—Jesus's arms are open to you.

Do you remember what it was like when you were little and you used to snuggle up in your parent's big bed? Do you remember the sense of peace and comfort you felt hidden away under their soft and warm covers? This is what Jesus offers to all who are weary that come to Him. He removes the heavy yoke from our shoulders and gently instructs us in the way we should go.

One of the awesome things about the kind of rest that Jesus brings is that it doesn't require that we drop everything and simply sleep the day away. No, the rest that God offers is much sweeter than that. It's that sense of calm even if you're in the midst of the storm. It's what keeps you steady when everything around you is shaking. It's the ability to not be anxious for anything when time seems to be running out. Rest for your soul means that your emotions get to be tucked away under the blanket of God's protection and provision. Draw near to Jesus today and taste how sweet His rest can truly be.

Your WALK:

If you are walking around with unnecessary burdens, take the time to pray and ask the Lord to remove them from you. Ask Him to show you what His kind of rest feels like and then walk it out.

HEART TRANSPLANT

The WORD:

*"And I will give them **one heart**, and a **new spirit** I will put within them. I will remove the heart of stone from their flesh and give them a heart of flesh."*

Ezekiel 11:19, ESV

The WORK

A heart of stone is one of the symptoms of a sin-sick soul. Someone with a heart of stone is typically unmoved by what's going on around them, and they feel no guilt or remorse for the bad things they have done. Have you ever met someone like that? Would you believe that this actually describes who you were before you met Jesus?

There was time in all of our lives when the Holy Spirit would attempt to tug at our hearts and we would shut Him out. The dangerous thing about shutting the Holy Spirit out is that the more we do it, the harder our heart becomes. This process continues until the heart becomes entirely hard, and nothing the Holy Spirit does gets through to us.

And therein lies the beauty of the transformation that the salvation of Jesus brings. He takes our cold, hard hearts and replaces them with hearts of flesh; hearts that are able to respond to the movement of the Holy Spirit. Hearts that have compassion for people you used to judge. Hearts that love people that hurt and abused you. Hearts that are capable of opening wide and allowing more love to flow to God's people. It's His gift to us, but it's up to us to keep it in good condition.

Your WALK:

As a follower of Christ, there will be times when He will ask to do things that you won't want to do. Don't shut Him out. Don't risk returning your heart to a hard state, but ensure that is always open and ready to receive from Him. You don't want to miss out on what the Holy Spirit has to offer.

MAKE UP YOUR MIND

The WORD:

"Elijah challenged the people: 'How long are you going to sit on the fence? If **God** is the real God, **follow him**; if it's Baal, follow him. **Make up your minds**!'"

1 Kings 18:21 MSG

The WORK:

Matthew 6:24 tells us that no one can serve two masters. We must choose one or the other. Many of us today are in a constant state of indecision. We have made the decision to become a follower of Christ, yet we waffle between living according to the principles of Christ and following culture or even our own desires.

In today's scripture, the people Elijah was addressing were the Israelites, the children of God. By name they belonged to God, but by deed they worshipped other gods, specifically an idol named Baal. God had performed numerous miracles on their behalf, yet they still had their doubts. In our own lives we have seen the Lord do mighty things, and yet we may find ourselves doubting that His word is true for us, or our specific set of circumstances. We even question if living this way is the best decision for our lives since everyone else appears to be getting ahead and living however they choose to live.

Whenever people say one thing to one person and something else to another, we call them "two-faced". Those people can't be trusted because we never can have confidence in which way they will go. Our lives in Christ are to be rooted in faith, and faith does not waver. It hopes and believes regardless of whether or not the proof is seen. If we don't want to be seen as two-faced Christians, then we must choose today how we will live everyday.

Your WALK:

Are there any areas of your life where you feel you are prone to waver in your faith? Write them down and then write down all the times that you've seen God come through in those areas. Remind yourself of His faithfulness and let that combat your fear of making a commitment.

UNSHAKEABLE

The WORD:

*"I keep my eyes always on the Lord. **With him**
*at my right hand, **I will not be shaken**."*

Psalms 16:8, NIV

The WORK:

One day Jesus's disciples were on a boat in the middle of the sea. A storm was raging, and the winds and waves were throwing the boat around something fierce. Needless to say, the disciples were afraid. Then, Jesus appeared out of nowhere, walking towards them… on the water. He called one disciple, Peter, to get out of the boat and join him. Cautiously, Peter stepped out of the boat.

For a few minutes, he was actually doing it. As he kept his gaze on Jesus, He was walking on the water! But then the rushing water caught his attention, and when he saw how massive and angry the waves were, he lost his focus. He began to sink. Jesus saved him from sinking entirely, but not without turning the experience into a teachable moment.

In this life, as we encounter countless issues, it's easy to take our eyes off of Jesus and put our focus on the problem, but it's in the presence of Jesus that we find our security. It is easy to get overwhelmed by what we are walking through, but Jesus is urging you and I to not get distracted. I know this is easier said than done. It's hard to maintain focus on walking toward your goals when there appears to be a tsunami going on around you. But remember although everything around Peter was complete mayhem, his walk wasn't affected by it at all. It wasn't until he started looking at it and allowing it to influence his walk, did he sink. Likewise, your surroundings may be in complete disarray but you must insulate yourself in order to remain focused.

Your WALK:

In those seasons when the wind and waves are tossing you to and fro, write encouraging scriptures on sticky notes or notecards and post them all over your home. Surround yourself with reminders to help keep your focus.

UNDIVIDED HEART

The WORD:

*"**Teach me** your way, Lord, that I may rely on **your faithfulness**; **give me** an **undivided heart**, that I may fear your name."*

Psalms 86:11, NIV

The WORK:

One of the qualities that every Christian must have is a teachable spirit. We have to be willing to learn if we truly want to grow. No matter how good we are and no matter how long we've been on this journey of faith, we can never know it all, so we must put forth the effort to seek the One who does.

As we spend time with Jesus and learn from Him, we develop a deep sense of respect for Him. It's what the Bible often refers to as the fear of the Lord. This is when we begin to understand just how powerful He is, how faithful He is to use that power for our good, and how sovereign He is to know exactly what to do and when to do it.

Ordinarily, we have many things that vie for the top position in our hearts: people, material possessions, or ourselves. But when the fear of God rules your life, nothing can take His place on the throne of your heart. The fear of the Lord is the beginning of wisdom, and a wise person knows who the king of their heart should be.

Your WALK:

Search your heart and ask yourself if you are teachable and if you have the fear of the Lord. If your answer to either of these questions is no, pray and ask the Lord to help you in these areas, as they are foundational to your spiritual growth.

NOT ALONE

The WORD:

*"The **temptations in your life** are no different from what **others experience**. And God is faithful. He will not allow the temptation to be more than **you can stand**. When you are tempted, he will show you a way out so that **you can endure**."*

1 Corinthians 10:13, NLT

The WORK:

As a small group of college girls were wrapping up their Bible study one evening, they shared a few prayer requests. Most requests were academic or relationship-based, but one of the girls felt like she needed to share a personal issue she had been dealing with... lust.

She said, "I know none of you guys deal with this, but I just have to get this off of my chest." After she had spoken, she was surprised to find that all of the girls in the room began to share that they struggled with the same problem, but because they each had believed they were the only one dealing with it, they had kept quiet about it too.

No matter who you are or how long you've been a Christian, you are going to face temptation. As disheartening as that may seem, it might do you some good to know that you are not alone. Some temptations are pretty common in our culture: sex, power, drugs, money, etc. Despite how common these temptations are, dealing with them is always rooted in shame and secrecy. Shame is what keeps us from escaping their grasp for two reasons.

1. Shame keeps you from receiving forgiveness from God. (1 Joh 1:9)
2. Secrecy hinders your sister's ability to lead you to restoration. (Gal 6:1)

No matter how bad things may seem or how trapped you may feel, God will always be there to show us the way to freedom and escape the grip of our temptation. Just ask Him to show you your way out.

Your WALK:

Is there an area of your life where you are tempted but have kept secret? Find someone to talk to and pray with about it. Chances are you'll discover you weren't alone after all. Afterward ask them to hold you accountable going forward.

GET OUT OF THE OUTCOME

The WORD:

*"**Commit** to the Lord **whatever you do**, and **he will establish** your plans."*

Proverbs 16:3, NIV

The WORK:

Control. Whether we realize it or not, we all want it. Some of us may even be *freaks* about it. If we can't get a situation to fit our exact specifications, we flip. For women especially, the desire to have things go the way we want, when we want can be difficult to reconcile with God's desire for us to commit everything we do to Him.

There is so much in this world that is beyond our control, but there is one who has authority over it all. To commit all you do to Him is to say, "God, I've done as much as I can here. I've kept up my end of the deal, now the rest is up to you." It's realizing that although we have our given responsibilities, we ultimately operate in partnership with our Father. This partnership is unparalleled because we are joining forces together with the one that will establish your plans and bring them to fruition. Who better to hand over your blueprint to than the MASTER builder?

Even if His timing and strategy look different than yours, you have to realize that you can't execute alone. Just do your part and let God take care of the rest. Focus on your input and let him handle the outcome.

Your WALK:

Ask the Holy Spirit to make you aware of any areas of your life where you may be manipulating situations to work out the way you want them to without trusting God to take care of them. Jot them down on a list and release them to Him in prayer. Now rest in the fact that nothing is too difficult for Him and watch God work.

The WORD:

*"Without **wise leadership**, a nation falls; **there is safety** in having many advisers."*

Proverbs 11:14, NLT

The WORK:

There's a sad story in 1 Kings 12 about an Israelite king named Rehoboam. His father had passed away, leaving the throne to him. Shortly after Rehoboam became king, the people came to his courts and requested that he be kinder to them than his father had been.

Rehoboam went to the elders for advice, and they encouraged him to listen to the people and to become a servant to them. But when he asked some of the friends he had grown up with for advice, they told him to be crueler than his father had been in order to keep the people in line. Rehoboam ended up following the advice of his friends and as a result was directly responsible for the division of the twelve tribes into two separate factions.

As you're starting out on your faith journey, you're going to have many questions. You don't have to try to figure them out on your own. There are many believers who have already been where you're trying to go. There are women that are more mature in their faith walk and have already experienced so much of what you are going through. Don't be afraid to go to them and draw from their well of wisdom. Seek the advice of such people and ask as many questions as you can of them. You will discover a safety net in sound counsel. I have avoided many pitfalls and been alerted to potential blind spots simply by asking for advice. Don't let pride keep you from opening your ear to another viewpoint. Wisdom from a seasoned believer can save you a lot of heartache, headache and wasted time in the end.

Your WALK:

Ask the Lord to direct you to some older women in your church or community that can be spiritual mentors or advisors to you. Spend time developing a relationship with them and allow them to pour into your life.

MIND YOUR MIND

The WORD:

*"**Fix your thoughts** on what is **true**, and **honorable**, and **right**, and **pure**, and **lovely**, and **admirable**. Think about things that are **excellent and worthy of praise**."*

Philippians 4:8, NLT

The WORK:

Part of the curse of our fallen nature is that our hearts and minds are prone to get us to do things that don't please God. Children are a great example of this. I don't believe anyone has sat down and rehearsed telling lies with their child or instructed them on ways to disobey. Children don't have to be taught to act that way, its just part of their nature. It's part of our nature.

That is why it is so important that we choose to take control of our thoughts. The Bible tells us that we practically have to beat our bodies into submission, when it comes to choosing the way of Christ (1 Cor 9:27). It's no different with our minds. The things that we think about can easily turn into the things that we do, so we must be diligent about guarding our minds.

When someone divulges negative information to us about someone and our first response is to think about whom we can share it with or we rush to a judgment call, we have a choice to make. Will we spread the negative or fix our thoughts on what is true, honorable, right, pure, lovely, and admirable? The choice is yours, chick. Make it count.

Your WALK:

Memorize this scripture and use it as a guide to test your thoughts against the Word. Whenever you feel a thought arise that it contrary to God's Word, check it against this scripture. If it doesn't fit any of the criteria outlined in the verse, chuck it!

PRAYER PAUSE

__Loving Father__, I seek your face for guidance and wisdom. Since you know the end from the beginning, you know how to move me forward. I need you in every part of my life. I may not see the results overnight but I can be certain that you will never let me down. You delight in your daughters calling on you and depending on you for all their needs. You are never too busy and long for your daughters to seek you. So I relax in your promises and commit all my plans to you because I know that you care for me. Amen.

JESUS CHRIST, CEO

The WORD:

*"**Work** willingly at whatever you do, **as though** you were working **for the Lord** rather than for people."*

Colossians 3:23, NLT

The WORK:

As Christ's role models to the world, we are called to be living stories of what a life filled with the Spirit is supposed to look like. Aside from bearing the fruit of the Spirit (Gal 5:22), we are to live a life above reproach; essentially the kind of lifestyle that makes it hard for people to find dirt on you.

One of the areas where it can be a little difficult to maintain the lifestyle of a role model is at work. Days may come when you don't feel like working, so you either skimp on the amount of time spent at work, catch a few winks when you think no one is looking, or put in less effort on projects than you know you should.

It's easy to fall into such routines when you're working for someone that you don't like or respect, but what if Jesus was your boss? How would that impact your behavior? The truth is that Jesus is not only your boss, but also the CEO, and even if your natural boss can't see how you cut corners, Jesus sees. So let that be a reminder to you to choose the path of integrity at all times. He's always watching.

Your WALK:

Have you been cutting corners at work or in other areas of your life? How will the awareness that Jesus is watching your actions affect your behavior? Practice living under the gaze of Jesus and see how it affects the choices you make each day.

QUIET CONFIDENCE

The WORD:

*"Charm can mislead and beauty soon fades. The **woman** to be admired and **praised** is the woman who **lives in the Fear of the Lord**."*

Proverbs 31:30, MSG

The WORK:

Back in high school, the type of girl that all the other girls were jealous of was typically the one that everyone considered to be pretty, right? If her looks could catch the attention of all the boys, she undoubtedly had the attention of all the girls as well. We all would want to look like her, dress like her, be her.

Throughout the ages, society has praised women who not only have beauty but who know how to use it to their advantage. According to society, the ability of a woman to use her looks to get whatever she wants from men is a strength. It's a skill that should be applauded.

But according to the Bible, the fear of the Lord is more important than charm and beauty. Why? Because when a woman knows to whom she belongs and understands how incredible that makes her, she begins to carry herself differently. And people take notice. If you've ever seen a woman who simply knows she's "got it going on", you know how admirable that can be. Let this be a description of you. Build your quiet confidence as you pursue the fear of the Lord in your own life.

Your WALK:

It's natural for us to look at the outward appearance and desire what other people have, but I challenge you to focus on building your relationship with and understanding of God so that you can become the kind of woman that other women desire to be.

CUT IT

The WORD:

*"So if your hand or foot **causes** you to **sin, cut it off** and throw it away. It's better to enter eternal life with only one hand or one foot than to be thrown into eternal fire with both of your hands and feet."*

Matthew 18:8, NLT

The WORK:

Now before you start thinking that the Bible instructs us to cut off our extremities if they cause us to sin, let me ease your mind. This particular verse is referring to the approach that all believers must have when it comes to sin. Anything that distracts you from God or tempts you to enter into sin should be cut off from your life.

A pastor once shared the analogy of sin being like a cancerous growth on someone's body. When it first appears, it is small and its "root system", if you will, is fairly shallow. So to remove it from the body would be no problem. But the longer you allow that disease to grow in your body, the deeper into your body it reaches, making it virtually impossible to remove without either causing damage to other organs or killing the host.

Sin is the same way. If you allow it to take root in your life, it will rapidly spread and become a force that you will have a very hard time controlling. That is why you have to cut it off as soon as it rears its ugly head. Don't give it a chance to destroy what God is doing in your life. Destroy it before it destroys you.

Your WALK:

What sin is holding you back from your relationship with God? Confess it to God and then write down three action steps you can take today to essentially cut it out of your life for good.

GOD > ME

The WORD:

*"**He** must become **greater**; I must become less."*

John 3:30, NIV

The WORK:

Before Jesus had revealed Himself to the world as the Son of God, John the Baptist had been the only one preaching to masses of crowds about the kingdom of God. Once Jesus showed up, people started leaving John and following Christ. Someone approached John the Baptist and asked how he felt about it. His words were, "He must become greater, and I must become less."

This is the perspective that all believers should maintain. When God gives us certain talents and abilities, the temptation is to take that talent and use it to get people to notice or praise us. But He didn't give it to us for that reason. He gave it to us so that we could use it to worship Him; to bring glory to His name.

Pride is our greatest enemy on this journey of faith. It's what caused Satan to fall, and it aims to do the same to us. We would do well to remember that if the whole world is staring at us, they can't see God. If we truly want to bring Him glory, we must humble ourselves and get low so that He is all that is seen.

Your WALK:

Search your heart to discover any areas where you may be trying to make yourself bigger than God. Confess them to God and make a point to pursue humility in those areas by pointing to God instead of yourself whenever the opportunity for recognition arises.

PRAYER PAUSE

Lord, let your spirit of peace soothe the innermost parts of my being. Cover every wound, every worry, with your everlasting peace. Heal the places where stress and anxiety have taken root causing physical discomfort and emotional unrest. Remove the 'fight or flight' responses that occur when I am out of sync with your peace. Where there is unrest in my life help me to trust you and to receive your peace which will surpass all of my understanding. Instead of dwelling on what I cannot change, I will apply your peace to every chaotic situation in my life through prayer.

Amen.

HEARTFELT PRAYERS

The WORD:

*"The **earnest prayer** of a righteous person **has great power** and produces wonderful results."*

James 5:16, NLT

The WORK:

Because most people like to break concepts down into step-by-step guides, let's take this verse and break it down a bit so we can get a grip on what effective prayer looks like. First, let's look at the word *earnest*. For a prayer to be earnest, it's got to be sincere. You really have to believe what you're saying and be eager in your pursuit of God regarding the matter. These kinds of prayers come from the heart.

Secondly, the person praying must be righteous or in right standing with God. God is not a fan of listening to prayers from people who knowingly harbor sin in their lives but act like everything's cool; therefore, if we want our prayers to be heard, we have to cleanse ourselves of unrighteousness through confession and repentance.

Finally, we're told in this scripture that when a righteous person prays in sincerity, there is power in her prayer and she will see good results. Sometimes we make prayer seem harder than it really is, but really it is just the overflow of our life in Christ. It's seeing what's happening in the world around you and feeling that the only way to solve the problem is by coming to God and then doing just that.

Your WALK:

Write down a list of the top ten people or issues that are most important to your heart. Commit to spend time praying every day for a week over them and see how God moves in response to your prayers.

MAKE FAITH MUTUAL

The WORD:

*"That is, that you and I may **be mutually encouraged** by each other's faith."*

Romans 1:12, NIV

The WORK:

One of the greatest features of books and movies based on true stories is that their ultimate goal is typically to use someone's life experiences to encourage others. Our life stories may not make it to the big screen or the pages of the next best-seller, but they can still be incredibly effective in encouraging others in the faith.

The apostle Paul said that we should imitate others as they imitate Christ (1 Cor. 11:1). Of course our first aim is to imitate Christ, but when you find someone who has a heart after God, it's not a bad idea to want to follow in her footsteps. That doesn't mean that you try to become them or lose yourself in their walk; it just means that you take those admirable qualities and use them in your own walk.

Just as you can be encouraged by other people's journey of faith, your life can also be a source of encouragement to others. The choices you make to believe in the Word of God above all else can speak volumes of encouragement to someone you never even knew was watching.

Your WALK:

If you're not already connected to a Bible study or spending time in the Word with a friend, do it! The time spent together, sharpening each other's faith will be an incredible source of encouragement for the both of you.

GOD-MODELED LOVIN'

The WORD:

There's more to sex than mere skin on skin. **Sex is** as much **spiritual** mystery as physical fact. As written in Scripture, "The two become one." Since we want to become spiritually one with the Master, we must not pursue the kind of sex that avoids commitment and intimacy, leaving us more lonely than ever—the kind of sex that can never "become one." There is a sense in which sexual sins are different from all others. In sexual sin we violate the sacredness of **our own bodies**, these bodies that **were made for** God-given and **God-modeled love**, for "becoming one" with another. Or didn't you realize that **your body** is a **sacred** place, the place of the Holy Spirit? Don't you see that you can't live however you please, squandering what God paid such a high price for? The physical part of you is not some piece of property belonging to the spiritual part of you. God owns the whole works. So let people see God in and through your body.

I Corinthians 6:19-20, MSG

The WORK:

As women, intimacy and connection is something that we crave deeply. If you think about it, we were created out of connection. Eve was literally pulled out as 'woman' from her connection to Adam's body. Most times we find ourselves in relationships where we use sex as a tool to obtain what we really want most... to feel loved, secure and connected.

The problem with sex outside of marriage is that it is partners with lust and not the God kind of love. So we end up with a one-sided exchange. We give up our most intimate and vulnerable sacred place and walk away empty handed. Of course we don't ever think it will be that way going into the moment because it is usually preceded with whispers of "I love you" and promises of togetherness forever. But what we must remember is that the void we attempt to fill with sexual acts can only be filled by the God-modeled love of unconditional commitment, sacrifice, and unity with the Holy Spirit. That kind of love comes from becoming one spiritually with your Husband.

Sexual sin is the only sin that violates your own body. It is self-inflicted against the very woman that God wants to dwell in and that He sent Jesus to the cross to die for. Jesus declared that your body, mind and soul were worth his pain and death and we deny this every time we auction our bodies off to the highest bidder for mere empty promises.

Chicks, we have to combat the lie the enemy uses to bait us into sexual sin in the first place. The lie threatens that if we don't give in, we will lose out on the guy and someone else who is having sex will win him over. If he cannot respect your commitment to God and your desire for more than hollow physical gratification, then you should willingly let someone else have him. Trust me you won't regret this move because in the end you will discover that a man that doesn't have a heart for being faithful to God's word, will undoubtedly also betray you.

I know you may be thinking that I don't understand the struggle since I'm a married woman. I see the messaging. The world is telling us women there is a shortage of God-fearing men, that competition amongst women is high, and you will die a lonely old woman unless you get in the game. Trust me I understand more than you think. Before I got married, I was a single saved young woman that didn't understand the price Jesus paid for me. I listened to the world. I indulged and as a result had a baby out of wedlock. What I desired from my boyfriend, I soon realized he was incapable of giving because it just cannot be achieved outside of a Godly union. Sexual intimacy was created by God and when enjoyed in marriage brings Him glory.

Your WALK:

Regardless if you are in a dating relationship or single, make a commitment today to glorify God through your body. Vow to remain sexually pure before God until you unite in marriage to the man that is ready to become spiritually one with you and the Father.

EVEN GREATER

The WORD:

*"The person **who trusts me** will not only **do** what I'm doing but **even greater things**, because I, on my way to the Father, am giving you the same work to do that I've been doing. You can count on it. From now on, **whatever you request** along the lines of who I am and what I am doing, **I'll do it**."*

John 14:12-14, MSG

The WORK:

The three years that Jesus spent doing ministry on this earth were filled with some pretty miraculous signs and wonders. He healed people emotionally, spiritually, and physically, and He showed His disciples how they could do the same. Then those guys ended up evangelizing half the world! Now, Christ has given us the same Spirit that His disciples had. Imagine the influence we could have if we actually tapped into what's been made available to us through the Spirit!

None of these works can be done in our own strength though. It is only Christ working through us that makes us able to change the world. All that we have to do is believe that God is the one with the power and the plan, and then make ourselves available to become the conduit through which He can perform miraculous works.

What's most important is that we seek to

understand what God wants. It's difficult to act on His behalf otherwise. Remember, the disciples had spent three years in close fellowship with Christ before He set them loose on the world. We must do the same if we want to see His power displayed through us as well. I once heard a Pastor say, "God must work in you deeply before He can work through you greatly." I couldn't agree more.

Your WALK:

Ask the Lord what His heart is for the people around you. Get specific and identify one person that you can minister to today. Yield yourself to God, spend some valuable connection time with Him and let Him work through you in miraculous ways to change this world.

ABOUT THE AUTHOR

Whether mentoring young women, hosting events, or connecting through small groups, Charisma Adams is wholeheartedly committed to spreading the Gospel of Jesus Christ. Charisma Adams is an ordained Pastor and the founder of Faith & Flyness™, a women's ministry on a mission to take over the world for Christ one stiletto at a time. Her ministry and work is targeted toward providing women and young adults with real, radical and relevant ministry. Her greatest joy is waking up every day as the sidekick to a Super Man (Jamie) and mother to three future world changers (Jamie Jr, Zuri & Reese).

Learn more at faithandflyness.com

CPSIA information can be obtained
at www.ICGtesting.com
Printed in the USA
LVHW010929120920
665767LV00050B/3069

9 780692 778890